This Book Belongs To: